7067 x

DISCARDED

The Freight Train Book

The Freight Train Book

Jack Pierce

Carolrhoda Books, Inc., Minneapolis

Special thanks to Burlington Northern Railroad and to John Burgandy of Soo Line Railroad of Minneapolis.

Grateful acknowledgment is given to Soo Line Railroad for permission to use the following photos: the gantry crane and This truck will drive away, from the Piggyback Cars page; Welding the steel floor and Loading boxcars, from the Boxcars page; Hopper cars carry loose materials, The rocks between the railroad ties, Loading an open-top hopper, and Hopper cars are loaded from the top, from the Hopper Cars page, and A work machine inserting new ties, Sawing old ties, Lifting a motorcar, and This crane may be used on or off, from the Special Equipment page.

LIBRARY OF CONGRESS CATALOGING IN PUBLICATION DATA

Pierce, Jack.
The freight train book.

SUMMARY: Photographs and captions describe various cars of a freight train, including the locomotive, caboose, boxcars, hoppers, flatcars, piggyback cars, refrigerator cars, tank cars, and auto carriers.

1. Railroads—Trains—Juvenile literature. [1. Railroads—Trains] I. Title.

TF580.P53   625.2   79-91307
ISBN 0-87614-123-8   lib. bdg.

1   2   3   4   5   6   7   8   9   10   86   85   84   83   82   81   80

to my niece, Cara

Locomotives

Engine cooling fans

The warning bell

The warning light and horn

Each locomotive has
a different number.

3,000-gallon diesel fuel tank

Engineer's Cab

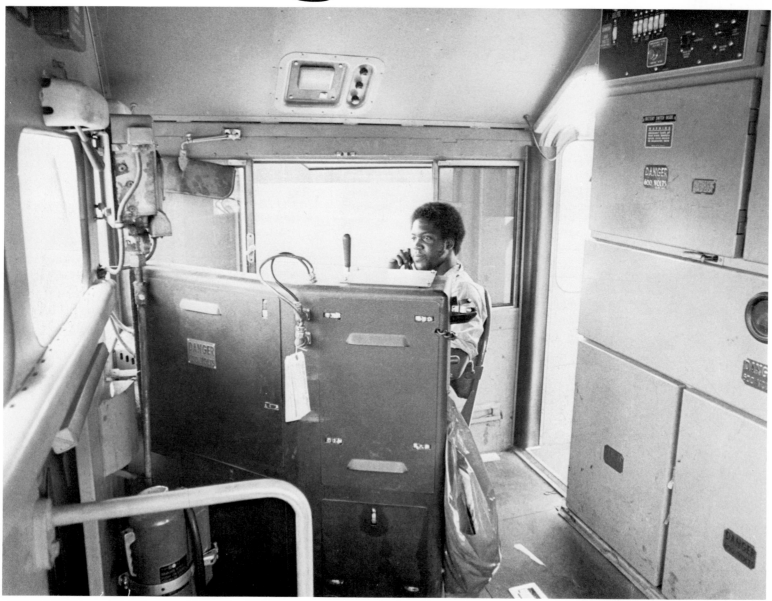

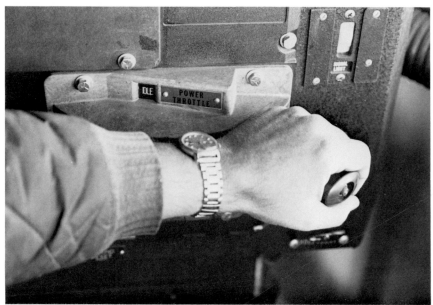

The engine power throttle

Buttons, levers, switches

The main control panel

A pressure gauge

Couplers

Looking down on two joined couplers. Couplers connect one car with the next. The wheel at the right is not part of the coupler; it is the brake wheel.

Couplers fasten automatically when one car bumps into another. The crooked rod connected to the coupler is called the uncoupling lever. Pulling it will release the couplers.

New couplers not yet attached to cars

Brakes are usually applied on all cars at once from the engineer's cab or the caboose, but individual brakes may be applied by turning the brake wheel at the end of each car.

Boxcars

Boxcars protect their cargoes from the weather.

Inside an empty boxcar

Loading a boxcar. These boxes contain model cars.

Welding the steel floor is part of building a new boxcar.

An old wooden boxcar

All cars have springs to help cushion bumps.

Tank Cars

LIQUEFIED
PETROLEUM GAS

Tank cars carry liquids like molasses, vegetable oil, and printers' ink.

This tank car has a ladder and a brake wheel on the end.

Tank cars are loaded through top hatches and unloaded near the bottom.

This tank car has three compartments.

The top hatch of one compartment

Auto Carriers

Cars and trucks are held securely with chains.

Ramps are used to load and unload cars.

Hopper Cars

Hopper cars carry loose materials like fertilizer and rock. This car is being loaded with grain.

The rocks between the railroad ties are dropped from a hopper.

Loading an open-top hopper car

Hopper cars are loaded from the top and unloaded from the bottom.

Some hopper cars have covered tops. Covered hopper cars have different top hatches.

Flatcars

Flatcars carry many cargoes: tractors . . .

railroad ties . . .

utility poles . . .

railroad car wheels.

more tractors . . .

The cargoes
are held on
with chains.

Piggyback Cars

Piggyback cars are longer than flatcars and have special fasteners to attach trailers.

This truck will drive away and leave its whole trailer on the piggyback car.

Some cars are loaded differently. This container will be lifted from its trailer by a gantry crane . . .

. . . and placed on a piggyback car.

Refrigerator Cars

Unloading a refrigerator car

Insulated doors help keep the car cold inside.

The cooling unit

Refrigerator cars help keep food fresh.

Special Equipment

This crane helps untangle and lift derailed cars.

A work machine inserting new ties

This is a snowplow.

Sawing old ties for removal

Lifting a motorcar

This crane may be used on or off the tracks.

A Trackmobile for moving cars a short distance

Cabooses

Conductors and brakemen ride in cabooses.

When the caboose wheels are moving, they turn these wheels which operate a generator that provides electricity inside the caboose.

The chimney for the heat stove inside

The cupola is where the conductor and brakeman sit.

Inside Cabooses

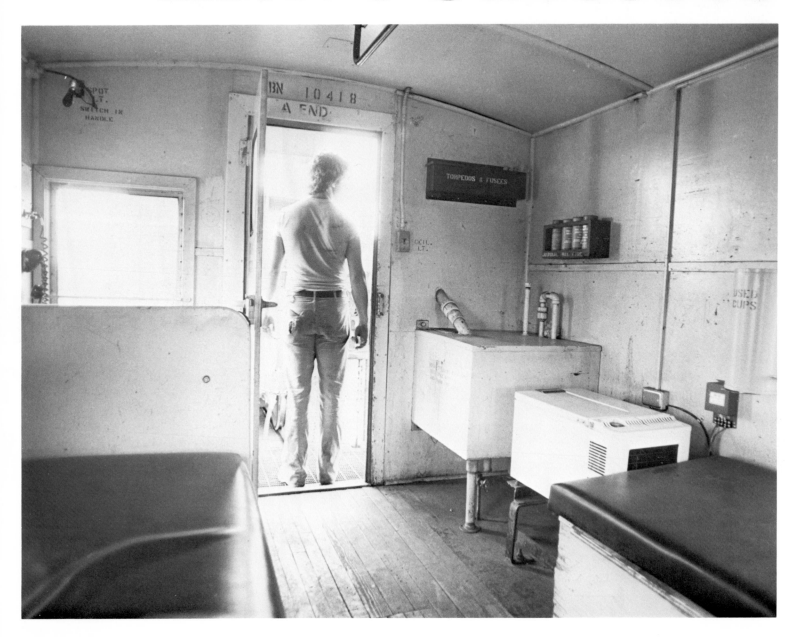

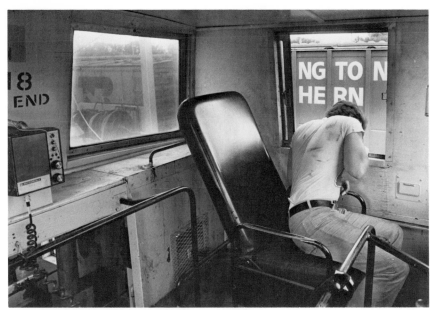

This brakeman is in the cupola.

Fixing the heat stove

Climbing up to the cupola

Chemicals are used to put out fires.

A radio is used to talk to the engineer.

The air release valve

Air pressure gauge for the air brakes

The End